T0160605

Objects For A Fog Death

also by Julie Doxsee

Undersleep (2008)

Objects for a Fog Death
by Julie Doxsee

Black Ocean
Boston · New York · Chicago

Copyright © 2010 by Julie Doxsee

Black Ocean
P.O. Box 52030
Boston, MA 02205
blackocean.org

Cover Design by Denny Schmickle
dennyschmickle.com

ISBN 978-0-9777709-4-6

Doxsee, Julie.
  Objects for a fog death / Julie Doxsee.
    p. cm.
  "Selections from this manuscript were first published as a chapbook Fog Quartets (horse less press, 2007)."
  ISBN 978-0-9777709-4-6
  I. Title.
  PS3604.O9545O25 2010
  811'.6--dc22
                                        2010005665

Printed in Canada

FIRST EDITION

Acknowledgments

Thanks to the editors of the following journals in which earlier versions of poems in this manuscript first appeared: *Sawbuck Poetry, Effing Magazine, RealPoetik, Copper Nickel, Unpleasant Event Schedule, Handsome, Cranky.*

Selections from this manuscript were first published as a chapbook *Fog Quartets* (horse less press, 2007).

"Lets Build an Empire We'll See How it Ends" is from Benoit Pioulard.

For inspiration, encouragement, and support, additional thanks to: Janaka Stucky, Carrie Olivia Adams, Mathias Svalina, Zachary Schomburg, Jen Tynes, J'Lyn Chapman, Bin Ramke, Julia Cohen, Joshua Marie Wilkinson, and Solan Jensen.

Table of Contents

Secret Water Quartets

Thirteens

Objects for a Fog Death

Meanings of the Null

Wood & Waterwork

SECRET WATER QUARTETS

A Bit of Couch

The ides of September
ghosted me until I flew

back from my house
on an origami swan you

left on my knee when I
drifted. When you said

it's crowded in my little
world I unlocked my

cedar chest, took out
little globes by the hand-

ful & with them filled
my cheeks. You filled

my cheeks with tears,
remembering to touch

my hand when the spill
of ice cubes filled

the room, snowing us in.

Sky Letter

Streams, waterfalls, & little
moon-side cacti spill from

a box lined with lightning. Close
by there is a path leading to a huge

hole in the ground that looks like
the paradise you hallucinated

when the shoreline kicked
your ceiling. I used to

enjoy the disarming flash
you, at sunup, put in my eye

& the smell of smoke
you, through the canyon, exhaled.

Now balloons filled with
misread nightmares

swim up, searching for
the hand I can't close

my verb around.

Poet

On the drive away

from the mountain, a walnut
appeared on my shoulder &

you questioned the omen, not
noticing my wing. Squirrels

again mistook me for a tree & left
a piece of real tree behind,

I said. You said I should
call somebody about that

dialing my house for me.
The statue of an angel

answered & said
in an hour according

to my numbers the
wing will fall right off.

Ode

I took a fishing expedition in a little
yellow slicker I dreamt up when I was

five, handed you the list. You checked
it & your watch & said you had to

roll. Did you notice that round piece
of air eavesdropping like a blank

CD, the normal clothespin
becoming a pair of legs on tiptoe

before our eyes? Where did you
go when you hung a left? You

left vapor trails I tried to
tornado with my hands. In the

doorway I swept
clean lingers the black

glove that fell from your
voice when you gulped.

Metalhead

About the scissor collection.
Loose wingspans of you are

wall-birds not even close to lying
cupped in a hand, still there is

an unspread finger triggering
open the fear of cool rings.

My necklace is buzzing, or is
a tripwire of pins &

needles behind the lightning.
The film is introduced by

a piece of paper you
ran your edge over,

a swept drape of hair
you razed. If you lasso

this finger later in the day
I will slip you off.

Phenomenon

Ennui saw me on the plane
& recognized my hat from

years ago, mixing many moments
of long-time-no-see into

one comet-lit afternoon. Have you seen
the film of the raindrop rolling

up the dollhouse door? I will
put it on your lip as a souvenir. Last week

the leaves died, leaving ghosts the birds
hide behind. Other tailless animals

stare deeply at the comet till
it splits into twin balloons. You'd think

this rain would turn falling fire
to vapor & resurrect those leaves.

Metal Tour

Videotape the stone's surface
to catch the hole it left behind.

This is your way of testing
each slipperiness decorated by

bombs & touches. Sit in this
white leather chair that looks

like a white leather chair &
foot-rest your machine. Migratory

songbirds are now swept away
by the dozen by the dozen

false winds & you saw their
wing explosions through the

lens. Why aren't you a wing
explosion? Why aren't you

a lens? You are a goblin
of the mines whose name

was handcuffed &
hauled off. You are the spoon

on a cooking show I
smelled in my dream. You

are an old bolt drilled into
a cliff that was given

to my mother long ago.

Secret Water

I couldn't pull the word
into thirds because

it fell deep & landed
in my gut: see my open

missing-of-you trying
to mouth it. We fogged

windows an inch
thick, veins in the

room grooming
invisibly into twigs &

tributaries you
shocked. You shocked

me in the seconds
before your trick

of cloud-making
thundered

the whispers of fog.

Offering

Thank you for hand
delivering a new park

to the village full of
kids who believe dams

are good luck. While I was
shipwrecked I found

the edge of the map
where you built it

using sonar, triangulation &
lilies. I rolled up

this watercolor—decorated
with pieces of actual

scissor—of you cutting
the inaugural ribbon &

plugged it into a
hole so watertight

the effluvia just
puddle at my feet.

Where Kinds of Water Meet

As the fire you light on
meets sea-level & the

sky's birthday blows you
out, you may from your ice

floe watch me spill the
envelope full of sleep I

untuck from my
button. I want to

turn you into an intercom
jutting from the glacier so

that kinds of waves may
question these dead

yells I lip-sync to help
you. Why aren't you

an answer? Why aren't you
asleep?   I look all night

but you swim with flow
charts written miles from here.

Instructions for a Pageant

In a country
full of hoof prints

that look like U magnets
when shot through

the lens, pour swimming
pools of naptime

& nest inside
the party

on the air
of popped balloons.

Magnets, Please

Untangle my expensive wing

from this strange
piece of nighttime or like

I said I
will come
at you at

one of the wee hours
as I make light
saber noises

with my twig.

THIRTEENS

An Intoxication We Attend

The higher quiet of me
walks through smoke just to follow

your breath to your neck to see where it
goes. After stuffing handfuls of tailwind in

your mouth, I see a sigh's turbulence kill
our half-bodies at the door, each arm threaded

to its splitting hourglass. Will you make
a shadow puppet the shape of my voice

in my mouth after the geography
dies? You pull from under the couch

a red magnet & our hands above it fire
off lightning that deafens just before

all noise turns into an animal whose bones
dissolve. Swamped with short ghosts of

breath, we return nightly to see how this
thing to say could lead to an ocean.

Ocean Show

26 new letters hydroplane
the space between our

mouths. Somewhere
on a map my body

meets your fingerprint
on its way to the next

city, then you fold
it up. Your body is

a map of skin more
you than your skin.

Architecture

If lightning is just more
heat, where is the cyclone

to entwine us until our
veins take down all

the trees between here
& seven days ago? If I write

my address on your wrist
the fog will wash it off, melt

into more ocean until
we are only more ocean.

Let's Build an Empire We'll See How it Ends

Forget planes mistaken for
stars mistaken for clouded

planets leering forth. You were
brightened by the sound of

an angel biting you right
on the hour. Your

skull's lamp's filaments
flicker toward us behind

the camel-fur scrim out-
skirting the neighbor's

freedom rock. Set your
cloud to the kind of clock

vultures circle. I could know
you better I know, I could

paint, also, a rainy scene from
which to subtract my getaway.

The Opposite of Fire

The future is swamped with
the 100 years of things to say

we seal in a box to oxidize a
century. When I meet you sleeping

you watch me, with a crowbar,
return to it nightly to wait. Days

change color inside, an only
child's voice says from the back

of your breath. We sleep
on that voice as it kills us.

Our Child is a Vulture

Had we the chance to touch what
lives in the folds between each

bird, we would collect it, bring it
to a hill, give it wheels & let it freefall

to the arms of bigger angels. You see
my teeth inside your words, this house

you make for me taking over the city
one ghost at a time. Architecture grows

like a root until parts of my air meet yours
in the corner of the east wing closest to

the ocean you stand on, waiting to feel
walls vanish on your lips.

Unfold

The metal envelope
the blueprint fails to

label: It is where we hide
a weekend full of rooms

& in those rooms treetops full
of fists flying open to let words

out to be the hungry noises
you would whisper into my

mouth if the pretty
omissions died.

Perhaps You Can Sketch a Piece of Fire

Ever-enduring, like the
mountains poets eat. Now

that we intertwine, my
onomatopoeia suctions you &

yours me. There are eight
kinds of mystery to swaddle with

lion fur. There are seven, only,
kinds of lion fur.

Perhaps This Chronology Has a Twin

Conjectural because I saw the sun
shoemaking as he mused. You number

me as I cough up the magic air,
exhume the broken bits of what

I bleed. These are my grammars
freckled with lolling feet. Don't ask

how many track mud.

The Time Between Now & Duration

At least we climb around on
what poems do. There are worse

ways to encircle before mid-ground
collision & what we do's the least

showable, hands atmospheric. At
most, sky patterns tell us the clock

will say 2:19 most of today, paralyzing
bodies a minute.

Hotel

I think of your hands
carefully folding paper

maps into strange swans
you leave S-necked in

the elevator. Please. Folding
me into an S on the bed.

Poem

Within its paper are jagged

dreams accordioning from
objects seen only for how they make

eyes. Here on my shoulder-in-hand,
you awestrike the impact, give birth to

holdable echoes I see rooted to
your voice as it falls. I see no choice but to

sew myself up latitudinal, flip over
the page to scar what's underneath.

Press the Button Again & Again

If you will be
the slippery water I

will be the floor-
heaped scarf

to pick up &
wrap around

you neck
to foot.

Touchingrange

Sheeting weather piles in my open
hand, ongoing. People elevator the upward

numbers, shrink to specks as we lock
a broken-off kiss in the jamb. Wedge

under your wing my century of *do you
see a day full of envelopes fold?* Inside

an east wall, buttons press
against your wingbone till I feel

no difference between skin & the 13
siphons in our chest.

Threshold Part Two

Folding up

tight on the minute-hand at
our heels, you hold mid-position

a body at the hips to borrow silk
from the violin noise mirrored in

miniature each night.

13

Paint chips melt
into flakes. They're so

tiny because I
erased my house

with a broom. Would
it ruin us silently to

let the magnets do
their thing? My

overwhelm
overwhelmed over

night, so you'll feel
right at home.

Future

Adolescent buildings disappear
& the way we be in a place is

indistinguishable from the
way we be smoking at the edge

real cigarettes on a fake
landing, fake smoke over

a solid liphold slipping.

Invisible Sonnet

The world sucks
out of its way the

word. Thorns
flower from stones.

I mention this
mystery now

to stifle it as if
it were a body. Sing

what writes you
even if it's liquor.

Eat what sees you
even if it's *the rapture*

of the spirit. Who put
the deer in the

treetop? Who reads
those hymns of his?

Only you can walk
through the sphinxes

in your hands, magnet
the secret shhhh

created pregnantly.

Invisible Sonnet

You stop landscape
with eyebeams & fork

over two pieces of paper
each with a drawn-on

corpse. I love what I want
to do with them. Plant them

in my eyes. Under a cannibal
mask, you drop handfuls of stars

& delete most of the electricity
uprighting my neck. My neck

is here. Do you engrave it? Do
you shock it free?

I Pretend Your Hands

I pretend your hands

are the cleaved sunup
this morning's window hums

toward the width of my
animal syllable.

Seven Vultures Shrink to Specks

During the other night's horse
& buggy you smiled your

sting right through a fictitious cemetery
handing equinoxes over to enormous

birds who spiraled up to crisscross
river & bank from fleeting latitudes

to empty invisible words out in
their nests. It was intolerably good

to sidle up to you when our voices
slept, when the horses went

hoarse in slow motion.

OBJECTS FOR A FOG DEATH

A Just Solution is to Cut

When you left
to take a walk in
the woods, I went over

to the glass case, cracked
your code in two
seconds & fished

out one of the
sandwiches. One
by one I found

the tiny pebbles
you left under the
tomato slice & ate.

Plane Ticket

You are
a little book when

I take you by the staple
& make my fingers an

OK. OK, you are
a bird.

Why I Am Your Dream

The lemon-shaped
hole in the seam of

your jeans puckers
closed. In a room

made of riverbank,
they only want one

thing, you say,
sewing buttons

onto patches
of moss. *Sex*

I say. *Experiments*
you say.

At First a Kind of Steering

My friend wrote
a song about you
like a pillow to

eat. I wrote
a song about you
made of igloos

ears can't swallow.
Without a roomful
of rabbits melting

minor spoonfuls
in the dognoise, who
can swallow?

Dear Rabbit Costume

To answer, one time
I saw the sun fall straight

into the Atlantic Ocean off
Virginia's coast. It floated there

like a crystal ball for eels to slither near
& it was my sister's job to clean it up

with ten closet-loads of gauze pads.
What saddens me most is that

until today I have not considered
how closely related I am to straw

that has met its share of hooves, how
fire-soaked cotton does not, quiet

like medical waste, supernova
what's left of the sun. There

is another story about a bird
flying low in a clearing lined

with twisted ambulances, a large blue
endless eye watching freed balloons weep

upward like air-tears not salting
the salt water. There is a still-

going marathon trapped at the side
of the road in a buckled knee.   We

descend & climb trees using the "3 on"
rule, singing high notes together in a vertigo

blackout now that the sun is swabbed. 3 limbs on
the limbs at all times. After leaves, leave

your friend at my doorstep & I'll
make him a meal of roast moon.

Rabbit Costume Tour

We met when the devil

& his secret friends
ran out of candy, wrote

a play in which
you disguised you

as a small, small pony & me
as a strand of grass. Here

is the spot where a monster
snipped open your screen

& slipped inside to smash
your eye & drinking

glasses. Here is where
you dropped a piece

of sycamore bark
in the dust for a

litter of kittens to
hockey puck. Here

is where I first saw
who lives where kinds

of water meet, where
I became in the blink

of an eye a river.

I Prefer that You Push Me

Propped up in my
chimney on a needle's
ice shadow is the
little Christmas
tree you left behind,
so I will send me next
day air.

My snowcapped
door ships in a wet
hinge & a halved
binocular to collect
its under-
foot light.

You left a picture
of a moon-sliver
cradling an ice cube
& said I could be
the wide bay of its
flip side.

When Detectable, Divorce the Gulf

My friend B's dog
was eaten
by an anaconda

who was cut open
by a hunter & tossed
in the river in half.

We stop here to take
pictures of these
questions. Who is

the anaconda? Will
its head & tail drift
or sink? In which half

of the beast
is the best
friend of B?

Dewpoint

Up lookout
mountain I hydroplane,

an eye weeps
pony-colored tears.

Schoolchildren's teeth
fill with fog & a city's trick

knees cramp. I should
date pilots, double

then quadruple my
cruising.

Lightbulb

Like a baby bunny
in my mitten
you erected
a molehill
& bounced
up to jack-
o-lantern
the eye.

Toys for a Fog Death

The first time I saw it I had
already been crushed

by a house & was preparing
to stay shriveled, head west

inside the tin a little
boy wearing a red

suit put me in.
From the asphalt from

a smile-shaped hole in the tin I
could see, barely, the salt

crystals clouding up &
little rockets started to come out

of my right eye. When
one rocket had gone

& the next was on deck
another boy covered

my left eye with a cheek-sized
blanket that melted

right into my head.

The Solid Odd of Headlights

Six months later I
translated the swans' winter dance

from my window & blacked out
when the landlord vacuumed

electricity out with those cooled
versions of light & melted my reading

glasses upping the thermostat
2 degrees. I lined the ductwork

with emails you wrote from Alaska
& the heat thrums, now, on the low

moan linking serif to serif.

Kitchen Tour

Those are
finger thicknesses

squeegeed on
your fog in the form

of see-through
sphinxes.

Those are
orange juice spills

kissed on
to your knee in

horseshoe
nebulas.

Those are
moths leftover

from the mother
of all moth wars

belly up in
your sunroom.

Those are
old teeth marks

in the water from
when I bit

all the ice
cubes in half.

Falsetto

To paint this
rollercoaster

the color of
common sense

sail it oarless
over the rapids.

Dear Drowning

After I poured you
I wrapped you in

a little black coat &
washed the salt

water out of your
hair. You took 17

globes & cut them
each into 4 eye

shaped slices at
the seams where

oceans meet &
said relax

we'll wing these
into water songs.

VHS Tape

All movies
are about how many sighs

of relief it would take to
blow out a skyful

of coals.

Drowning Tour

Here is the place
beside his mouth
where he put up
his hand
to shout *hey, Frank*
with a voice
scraped from the
sea-green floor.

Here is Florida
facing him with-
out its magic lung
on the busy road
where lemons fly
out of trucks & leave
watermarks on
the sky.

VHS Tape in the Bath

The person who
saw a cat flood

the brickwork
saw a cat mistake

squeaking spigots
in the mouse-shaped

light. The psychic
who glued this water

onto the wall
could be close &

cool like the back
of a hand.

MEANINGS OF THE NULL

Xylem

Your bells
unyellow as they fall,

hollow out a song
to fill with splinters. The minus sign

on the coastline wants you, but in
January buses don't run

before a naked man brings
your stalk to where

his body & a snow
bank melt.

Halo

On this day
I take a bite of

glow & become
part of you. I eat

a fireball in someone
else's wooden yard.

When we fissure
smooth water

with fishhooks
I am handed the

legal pad of words
you hide in. You

are a lizard in the
headlight but I see

only angel & tail.

Februarying

Sullen hikes in the
ice cream snow

melt the new year onto
confetti the serifs

shrink. The word *year* is
curled up on a snow-blind

sheet or is typed onto snow
waiting for a large person's

angel-smash.

A Fugitive Thing Readily Ignites

The dead remove you from a

velvet sack with one hand
while licking fingerprints

from the fingers of the
other. This doesn't matter.

What matters is how
a handhold reddens but

doesn't leave the hand.

Skyholes that Made You Laugh

I throw a moon, it rolls
onto your bathroom roof.

Look where the sky greens
around where I ripped

it, full null hung
like a roar. Radios screw

up. I told the bullet
whir & the bullet

made a world.

Sill

Do you see

the biggest bouquet I
have ever seen in you

is nicest
at noon?

On every

solid wall I draw
a picture of fog &

glass it with
my glance.

Under the Covers Are My Flung Halos

Long after the whimper

animals leave, you place
one on my knee

where someone's
arm-flail said

you should.

Thank You, Window

At 98.7 the room
temperature baby-

sits a growing heartbeat
while sundown removes a

picture of late summer
like the acorn from a

squirrel's jaw. You
smell daisy-nice the piano

player thinks. He never
turns the page, but the music

changes every minute on
the minute. *I am drunk*

when I drink you is the
song that meets

the shatter.

X

With a fingertip you cross
my chest beginning to end &

we graduate gradually
to knives. In a trance

under the violet-blind sheet
I see only the wind

waving violets, cartoon-
ripe from a plan perfectly

cut. Tingling after the
grip, your hands make

a shadow parrot, but
there is no sun to cast it, to

make it look not guilty
like hands.

Birthday

In my yellow apart-
ment, daffodils wilt

& I fall northward
packing bones

back into my body
where the fore-

head sounds
shuuush out.

As Cut by a Hunting Knife

When a weathered star
falls from your t-shirt

our vision bleaches for a
minute & we sort through

the air with our fingers before
collapsing in the back-

lit shadows. You say
it is Western, everything

I know about moons
loosening occasionally

to bonk you.

A Song Unfolding

You are coming
to know the alive

as they stand like
a black forest, arm

a candleholder
for whimpers that are

pronged, not soft like
milestones. So why do you

think I'm quiet when
the water bulges like a howl

& your fingers undo
the bouquet?

Era

Whenever eyes go
above your head

I slip you a fireball
& wound it till it

halos. It's a big big
world: fire-mean, full

of blinking lambs.
I know you from time

to time lose foot-
steps in the

ocean, whisper
into my rib *I see*

you in the bits of falling
galaxy & breathe

you in till blind.

Shove

Long cinematic thrall
cycloning, animals

whose heads poke
from the dirt blink

awake to find a
magnet shaped like a

pair of hands to sit
in. Very pastoral, very *where*

did I put that tornado? A shoe-
horn, a silence. A place

to twist things up under
the late, late shadow of

a stone trying hard
to pinecone, a beak

trying hard to help it.

Standing Up with No One

Everything hisses,
grapefruits oxidize

a ceramic jesus
pulled from a

batcave. Of the
sorts of vine, I prefer

*di*vine. Divide
me the long way

so I'm no longer
double using a special

shatter-tool that
vivisects, perfectly,

the little statue
inside each ear.

WOOD & WATERWORK

Fountain

Your waterfront is so
like a day's supply of

satellite. You sonar my
wishes & molehill them. I find

a monocle on your cupid
& the smudge of a rubbed-

off antenna. I take
your stepladder all the way

to the middle where
algae sprouts in moon-

scapes to prevent showers
from splashing your sides. You

point up to the papers
waterfalling from

my coat & show them
the bends in your water.

Dear Sparrow

I live in a cave
exactly one

river long. Brief me
on the song

keeping time to your
flap. Yell out the

sex of the
crow baby. You

pretend my door
is your skyload

of leaves, a new
kind of air

you sail.

I'm the Canoe Eating Echoes

near water that sings *hi*

love me whenever there
is a near ear to hollow.

I sleep on my side, wild
cats up & down my

thighs, on & off until
nine lives hiss future

ghosts to life. From
here I see the sparrow

on your forehead
filling its tongue

with stems. From
here I see the bird legs

running a verb over
to wash it. Wish it. From

here I see yesterday perched
on my oar, extending an

invitation to capsize.

Long Lost Hallucination of Sparrow

To answer, you landed on my
whimper with a black-socked

talon & changed it to purrs,
then made a convex movie

of it on the teakettle. To carry
my boatload of films I needed

access to your little friend the
black horse. This is a picture of our

saddlebags bursting as we run south
on 6th. Each day the baby birds you swiped

help fluff my feather pillow with house-
broken beaks. We are sending pictures

of that irony in this little clamshell box.

Dear Woodwork

When I come out of you
I will have a small

dried angel in my hand & a
to-do list. Decades of

handymanning have
left a crescendo

of warped angles.
I was able to wedge open

a slant of light by tripping
your mechanism from beneath.

Under glaring colors, the
other side of you buckles

& painted-in angels fly home.

River

I dream you float &
become two of your

children who break
loose to soak a pail of

scissors. I put my
finger in my eye &

laugh. This birdcall is
the little door you went in

yesterday after kayakers
gasped for breath. This

bucket of you is cut
into raindrops & counted.

To the Less Accurate Rippling of Tunes

Here is the new tattoo
I found in your moss,

scar upright like a
wooden chair

propped on animal
pelts. Here is the vivid

memory of canoes
that left your head.

I see from bird's
eye a mailbox submerged

to the flag. My little
excursion to your neck

sandblasted every
bright thing till nude &

look, I'm holding
what's left on my tongue.

Ode

Your up-my-
sweater hand felt

the end
of the bandage &

a black glove fell out
of your voice

when you gulped.
Please take this piece

of paper with an index
finger drawn on it

in chalk. Unwrap your gold-
toe & let your big toe

unfold it, magnet it
to the fridge.

Seconds Before the Floorboards Fail

When I hear your wish, gates
unveil a dreamt poet

who walks up with an armful
of cut-off pockets. He is

your brother minus the tiny word
dividing his voice. Your sentence

has commas where shuteye should be &
the bed goes up in flames when

you wave your twig. I have seen
ears empty out on paper, sound

burrowed in the rough bark. I blame sleep
not the book in the pocket of my gown.

I was sure eyes touch. And you, asleep
beside my bones round the clock

wake to loosen fire
from its frame.